CONTEMPORARY MUSICAL THEATRE FOR TEENS

YOUNG MEN'S EDITION VO

26 SONGS FROM 21 MUSIC

ISBN 978-1-4803-9520-6

HAL•LEONARD® CORPORATION

7777 W. BLUEMOUND RD. P.O. BOX 13819 MILWAUKEE, WI 53213

Visit Hal Leonard Online at
www.halleonard.com

CONTENTS

RADAMES' LETTER

from Elton John and Tim Rice's *Aida*

Music by Elton John
Lyrics by Tim Rice

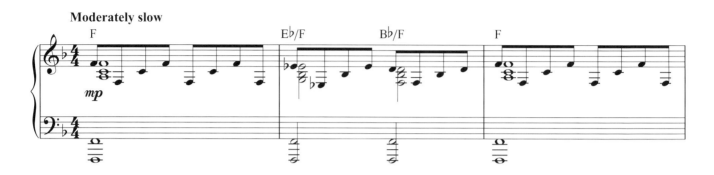

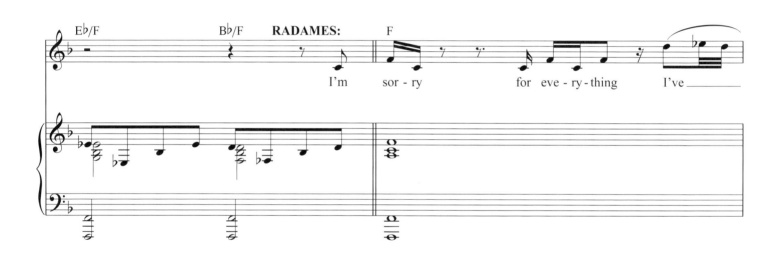

RADAMES:
I'm sor - ry for eve - ry - thing I've ___

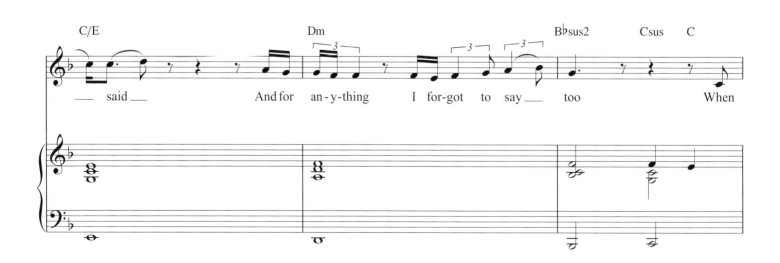

___ said ___ And for an - y - thing I for - got to say ___ too When

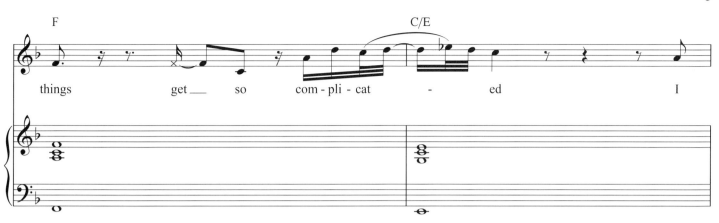

things   get ___ so   com - pli - cat   -   ed   I

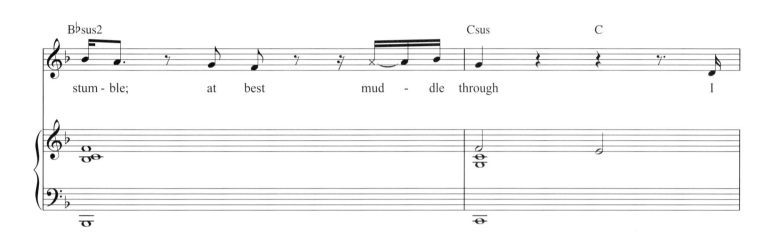

stum - ble;   at best   mud - dle through   I

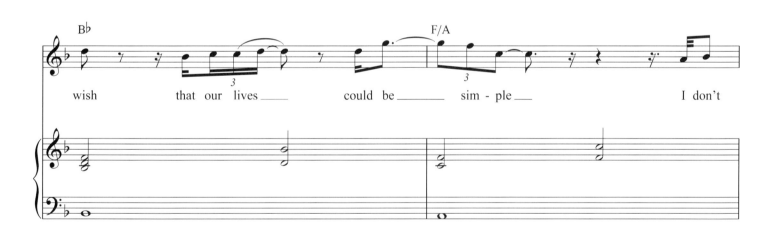

wish   that our lives ___   could be ___ sim - ple ___   I don't

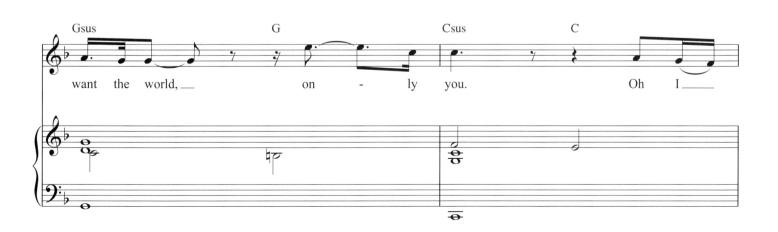

want the world, ___   on - ly you.   Oh I ___

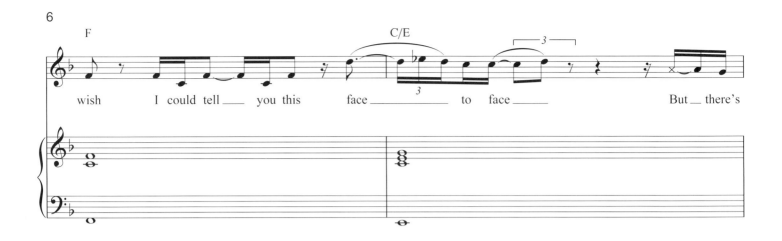

wish I could tell ___ you this face ___ to face ___ But ___ there's

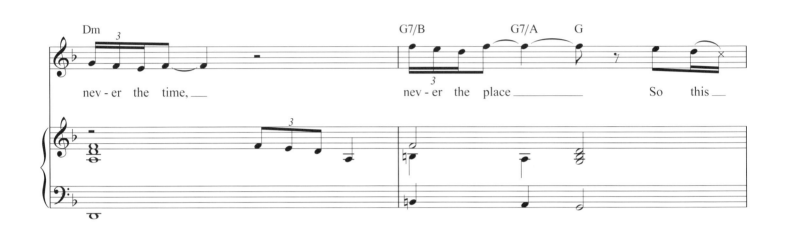

nev-er the time, ___ nev-er the place ___ So this ___

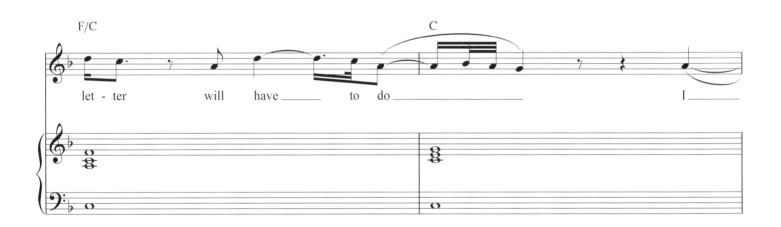

let-ter will have ___ to do ___ I ___

love ___ you.

IF YOU WERE GAY
from the Broadway Musical *Avenue Q*

Music and Lyrics by Robert Lopez
and Jeff Marx

free to ___ say that I was gay! (But I'm not gay!)

If you were

queer, I'd still be here, year af - ter

year, be - cause you're dear to ___ me. And I know that

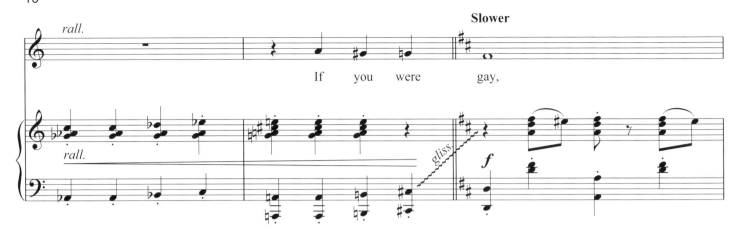

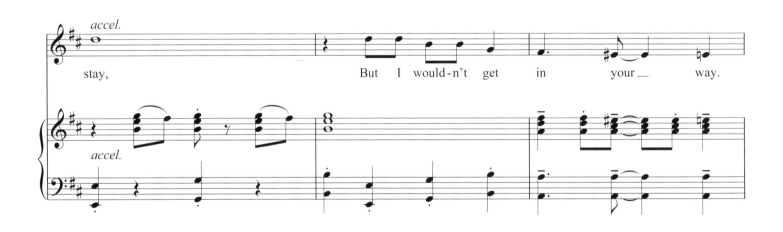

I'M NOT WEARING UNDERWEAR TODAY

from the Broadway Musical *Avenue Q*

Music and Lyrics by Robert Lopez
and Jeff Marx

Fast and circus-like

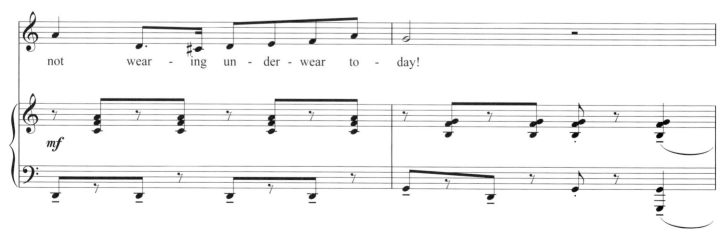

not that you prob - 'ly care much a - bout my un - der - wear,

still, none - the - less I got - ta say, _____

that I'm not wear - ing

un - der - wear to - day! _____

f

gliss.

ENJOY THE TRIP

from *Bring It On*

Music by Tom Kitt
Lyrics by Amanda Green

Driving mid-tempo Pop (♩ = 83)

RANDALL:

I'm a

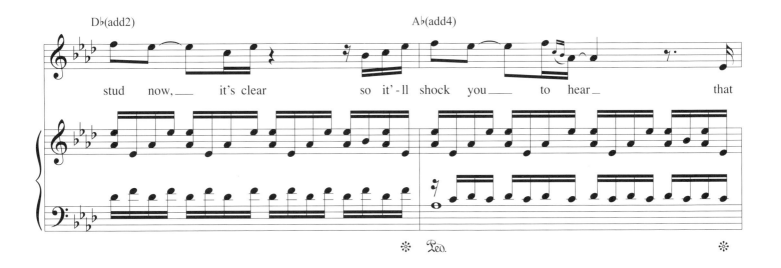

stud now,___ it's clear   so it'-ll shock you___ to hear___   that

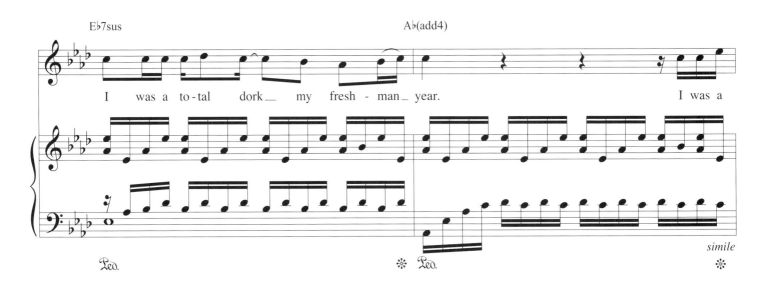

I was a to-tal dork___ my fresh-man__ year.   I was a

WHAT I'VE BEEN LOOKING FOR

from the Disney Channel Original Movie *High School Musical*

Words and Music by Andy Dodd
and Adam Watts

Originally a duet, this song has been adapted for this solo edition.

I've been look-ing for._____

So good to be seen; _ so good to be heard. _____ Don't

have to say a word._____ For so long, I was lost; ___ so good to be found. _

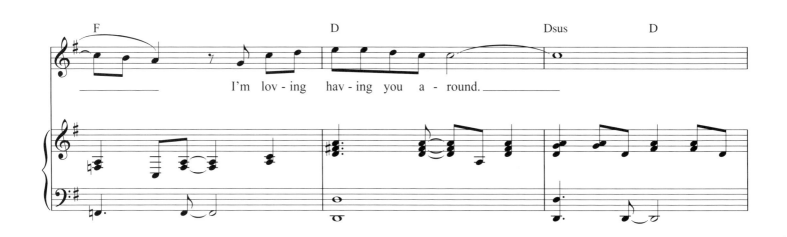

_____ I'm lov-ing hav-ing you a - round._____

LOVE TO ME

from *The Light in the Piazza*

Music and Lyrics by
Adam Guettel

no - tice how you hun - ger for sur - prise,___

and do not think that you are tall e - nough,

like you're stand - ing on___ a

moun - tain - side___ a - lone.___ This is what I

fore,_____ since that mo - ment in the

square_____ when your

hat is car - ried in the air_____

just so you can chase it,_____

just so I can be there. This is how I know.

This is what I see. This is love to

me.

ONE STEP CLOSER

from Walt Disney's *The Little Mermaid - A Broadway Musical*

Music by Alan Menken
Lyrics by Glenn Slater

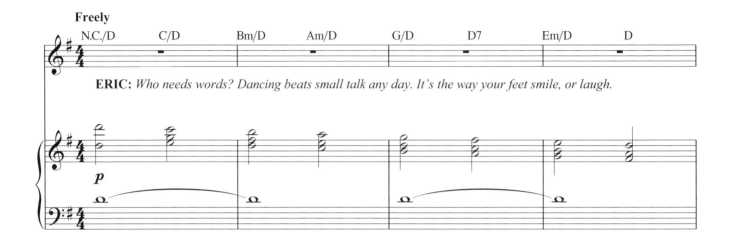

ERIC: *Who needs words? Dancing beats small talk any day. It's the way your feet smile, or laugh.*

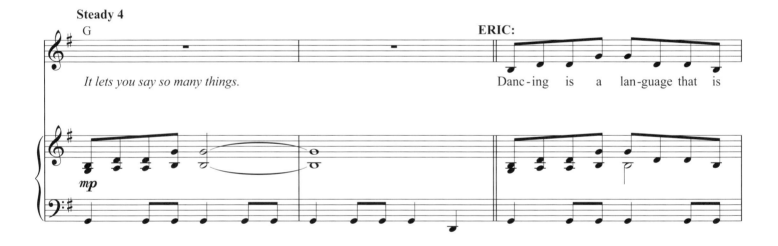

It lets you say so many things.

ERIC: Danc-ing is a lan-guage that is

felt in-stead of heard.

You can

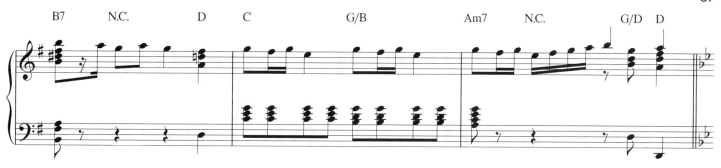

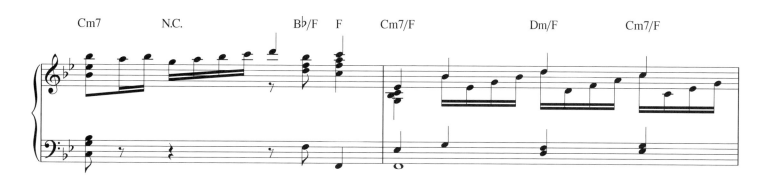

A dance is like a con - ver - sa - tion _____ ex -

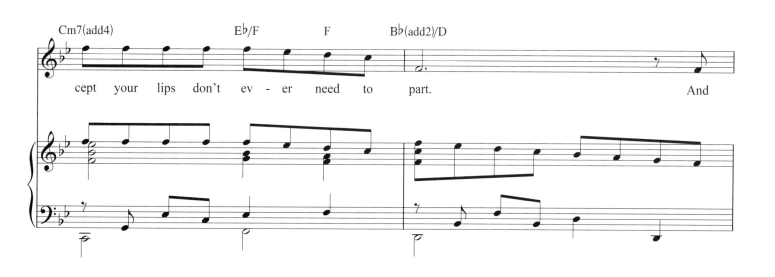

cept your lips don't ev - er need to part. And

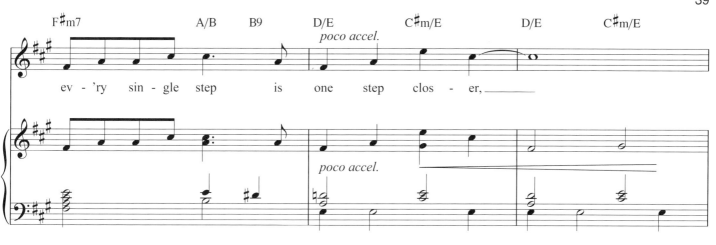

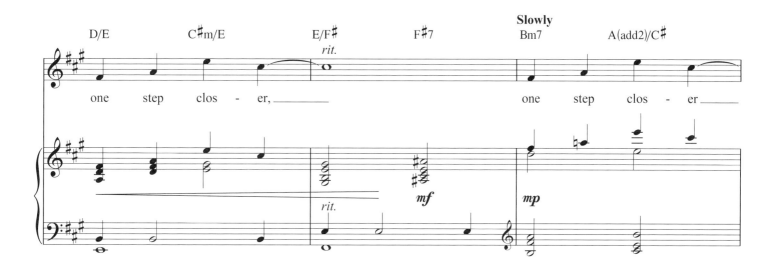

THE STREETS OF DUBLIN
from *A Man of No Importance*

Lyrics by Lynn Ahrens
Music by Stephen Flaherty

ROBIN'S SONG
from *Monty Python's Spamalot*

Words by Eric Idle
Music by Neil Innes

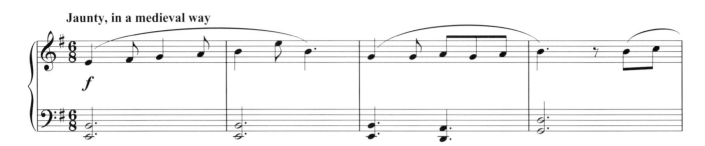

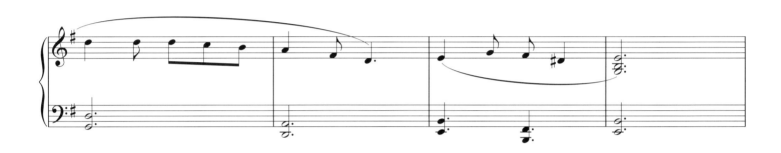

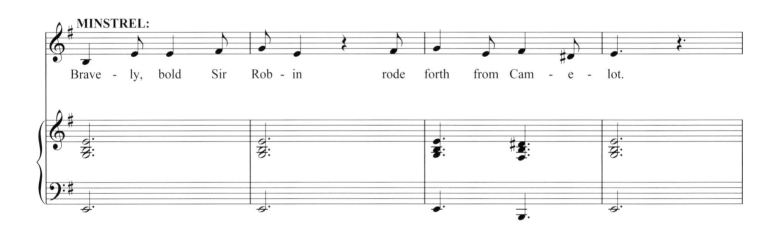

MINSTREL:

Brave - ly, bold Sir Rob - in rode forth from Cam - e - lot.

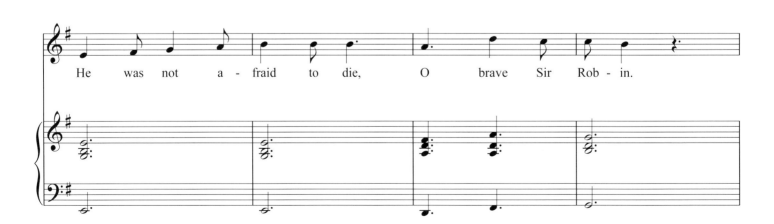

He was not a - fraid to die, O brave Sir Rob - in.

have his knee-caps split, and his bod-y burned a-way   And his
limbs all hacked and man-gled, brave _ Sir Rob-in!   His
head smashed in and his heart cut out, And his liv-er re-moved and his bowels un-plugged, And his
nos-trils raped and his bot-tom burned off, And his pe-nis split and his...   [he stops himself]*

* In the show, the song is interrupted by Robin.
  In this solo edition, the singer stops himself, suddenly realizing what he has just said.

I NEVER PLANNED ON YOU
from Disney's *Newsies The Musical*

Music by Alan Menken
Lyrics by Jack Feldman

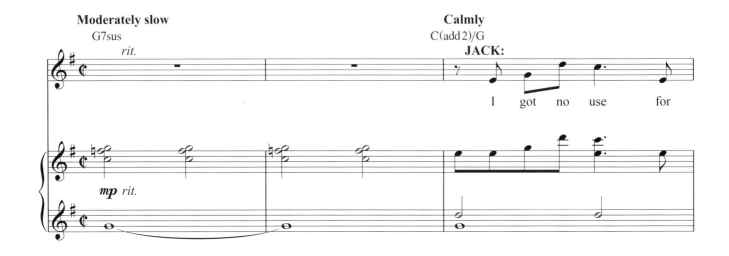

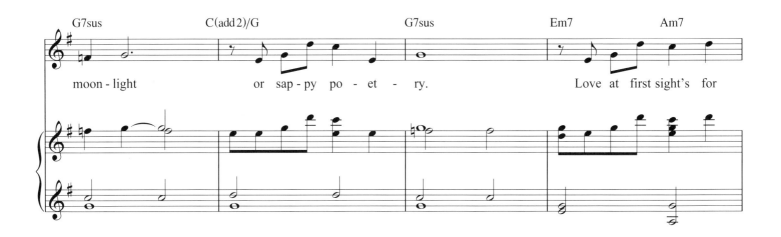

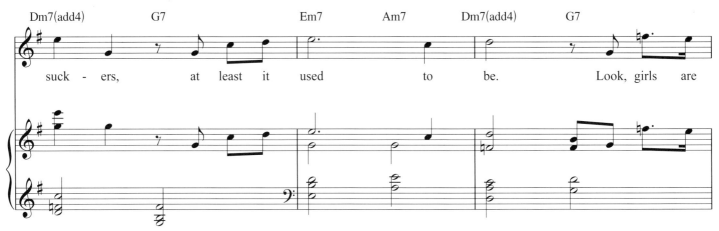

This has been adapted as a solo, eliminating "Don't Come A-Knocking."

SANTA FE
from Walt Disney's *Newsies*
(Movie Version)

Lyrics by Jack Feldman
Music by Alan Menken

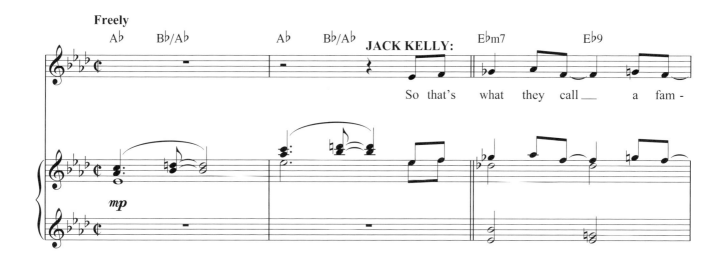

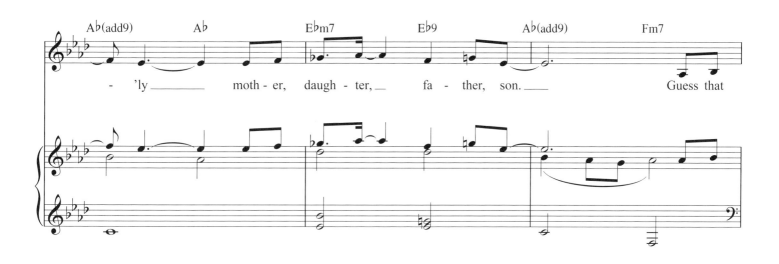

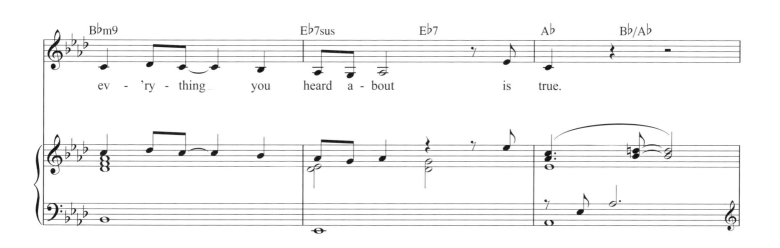

And I'm free like the wind, like I'm

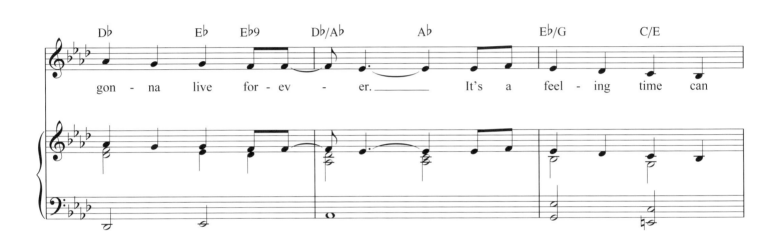

gon-na live for-ev-er.___ It's a feel-ing time can

nev-er take a-way.___ All I

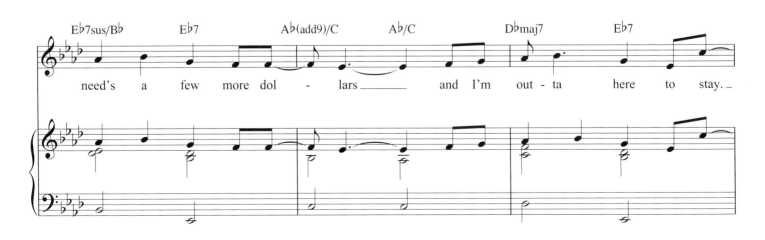

need's a few more dol-lars___ and I'm out-ta here to stay.___

Dreams come true. Yes, they do _____ in San - ta

Fe. _____ Where does it say you

got - ta live and die here?

Where does it say a guy can't catch a break?

Why should you on - ly take what you're giv - en?

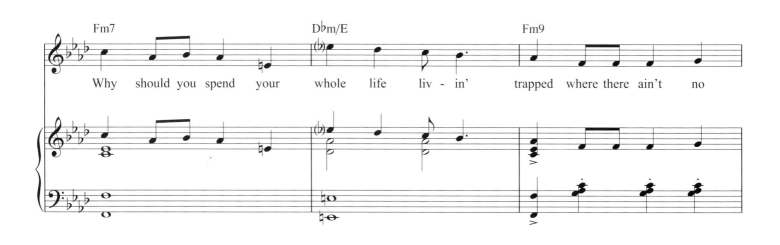

Why should you spend your whole life liv - in' trapped where there ain't no

fu - ture. E - ven at sev - en - teen

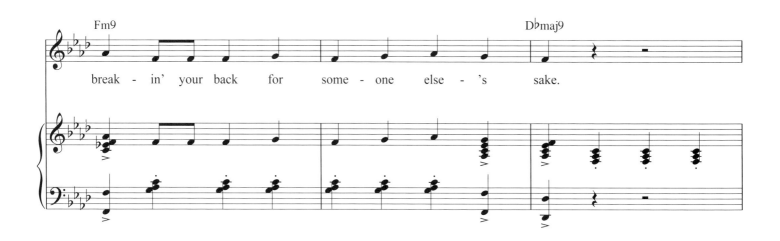

break - in' your back for some - one else - 's sake.

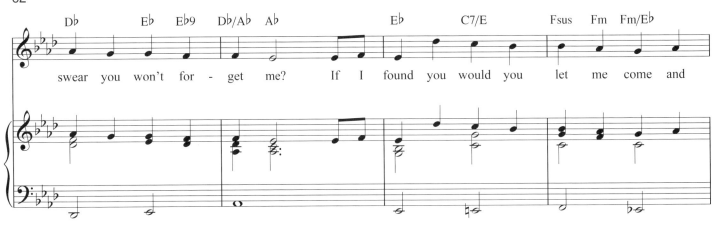

swear you won't for - get me? If I found you would you let me come and

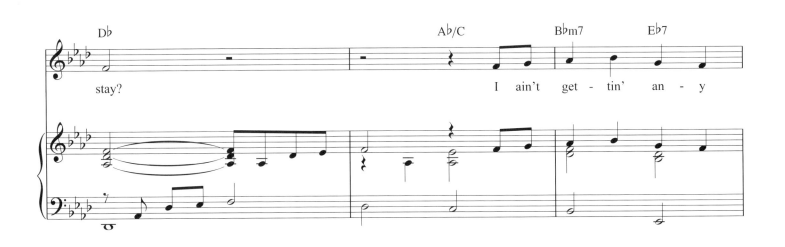

stay? I ain't get - tin' an - y

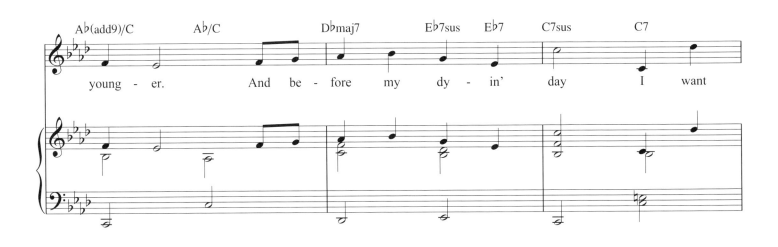

young - er. And be - fore my dy - in' day I want

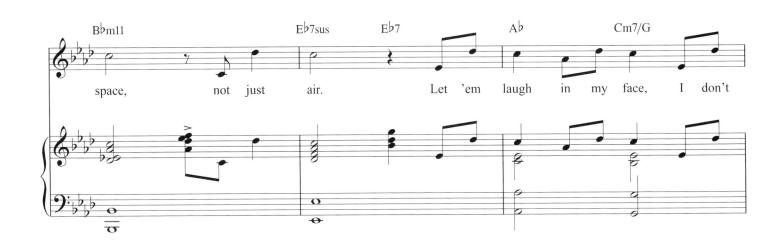

space, not just air. Let 'em laugh in my face, I don't

SANTA FE

from Disney's *Newsies The Musical*
(Broadway Version)

Music by Alan Menken
Lyrics by Jack Feldman

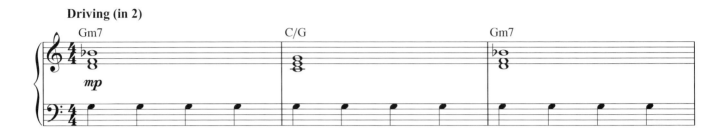

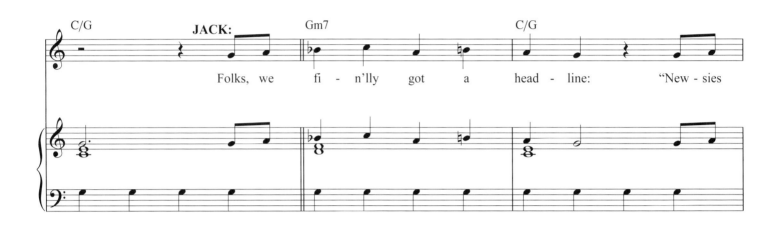

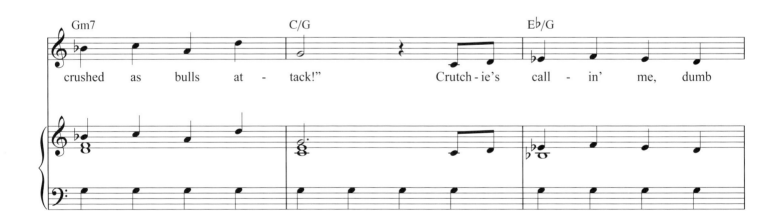

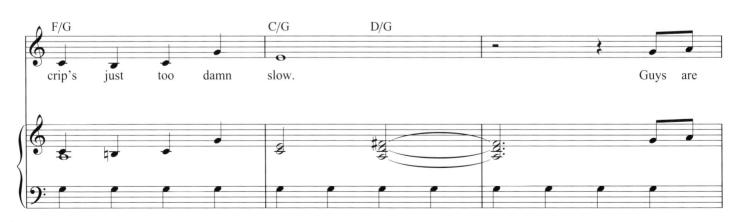

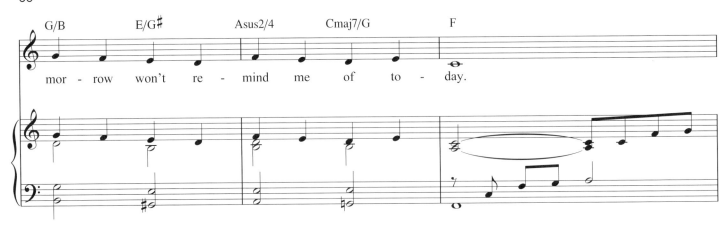

mor - row won't re - mind me of to - day.

When the cit - y's fi - n'lly sleep - in', and the

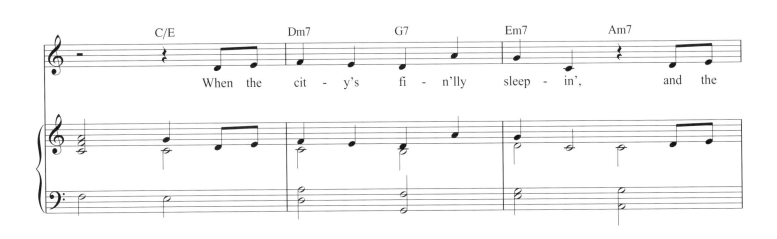

moon looks old and gray, I get on the train that's

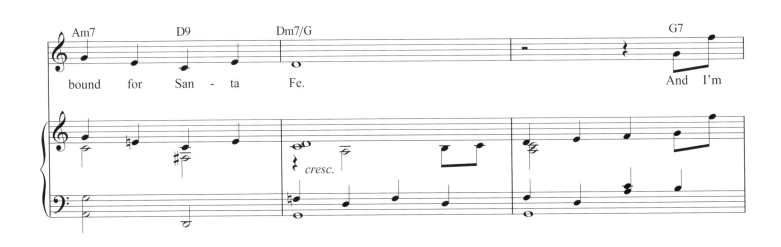

bound for San - ta Fe. And I'm

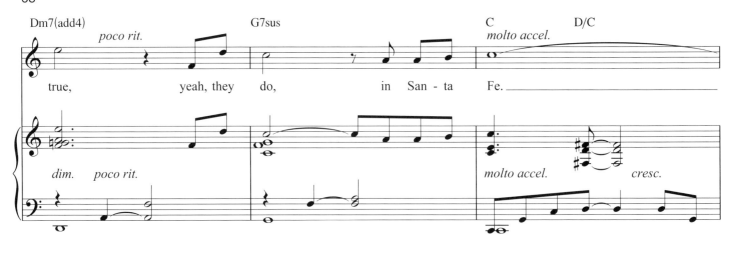

true,   yeah, they   do,   in San - ta   Fe. _____

With more drive

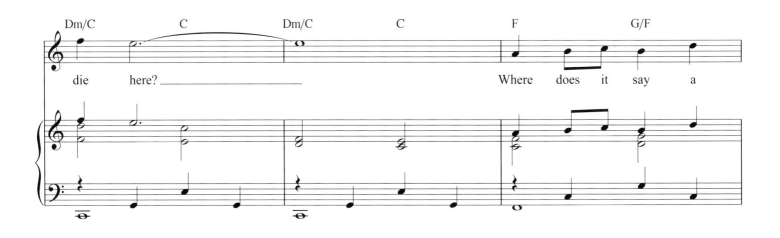

Where does it say you got - ta live and

die here? _____   Where does it say a

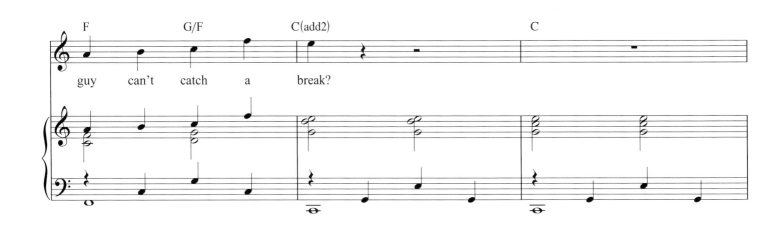

guy can't catch a break?

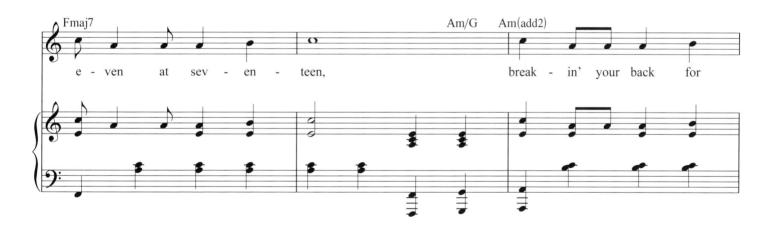

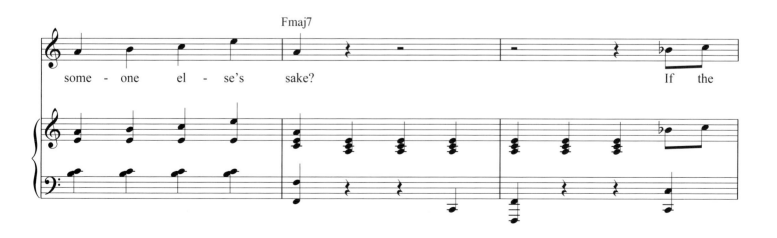

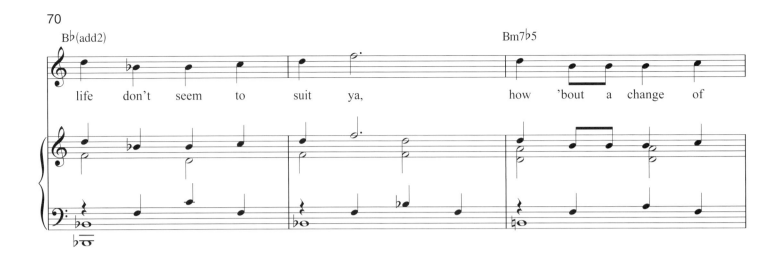

life don't seem to suit ya, how 'bout a change of

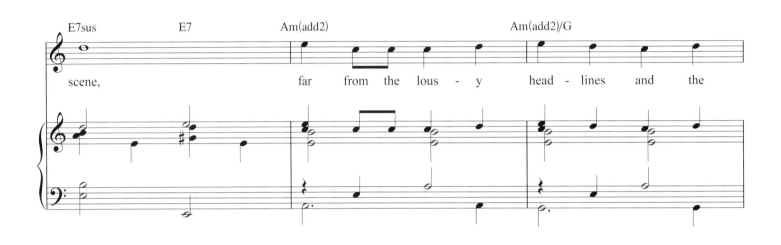

scene, far from the lous-y head-lines and the

dead-lines in be - tween!

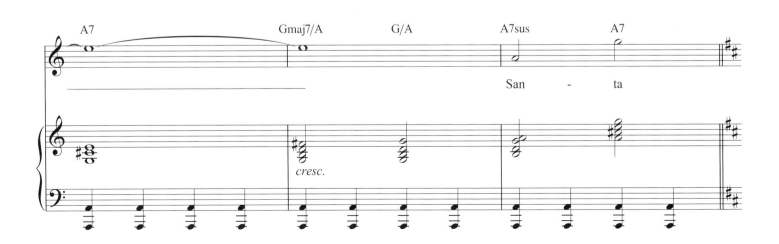

San - ta

More broadly

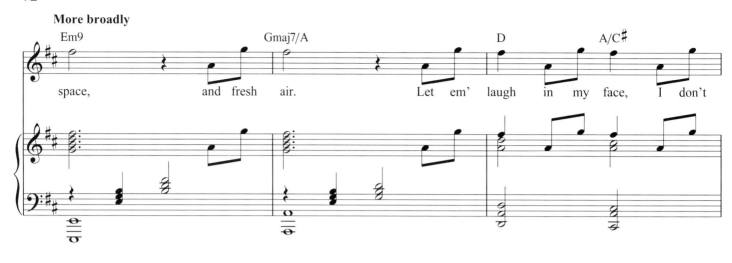

space,   and fresh air.   Let em' laugh in my face,   I don't

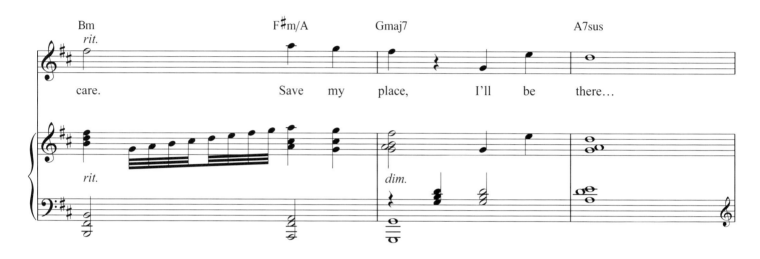

care.   Save   my   place,   I'll be   there…

A tempo (poco rubato)

Just be real is all I'm ask - in',   not some

SOME GIRLS

from *Once on This Island*

Lyrics by Lynn Ahrens
Music by Stephen Flaherty

YOUR EYES

from *Rent*

Words and Music by
Jonathan Larson

by sur - prise _____ the night you came _ in - to _____ my life. _ Where there's

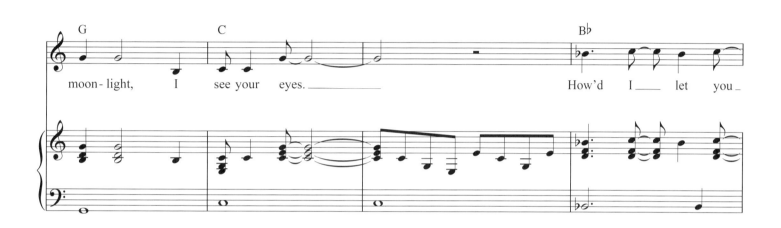

moon - light, I see your eyes. _____ How'd I ___ let you _

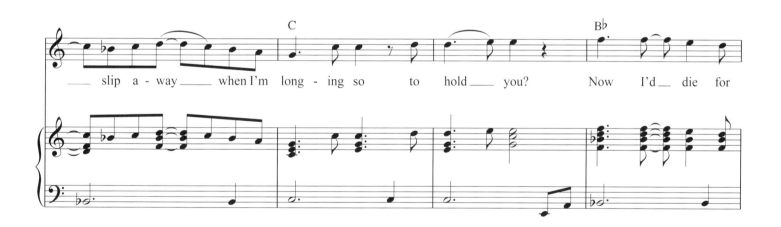

___ slip a - way _____ when I'm long - ing so to hold ___ you? Now I'd _ die for

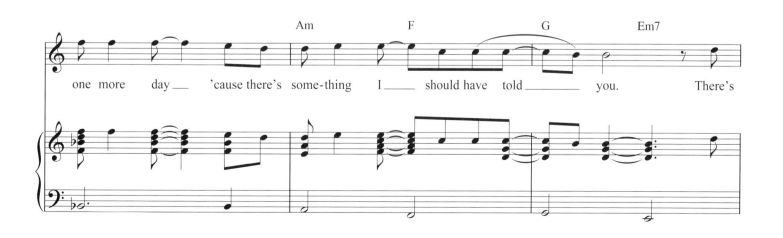

one more day ___ 'cause there's some-thing I _____ should have told _____ you. There's

something I ____ should have told _____ you   when I looked in - to your

eyes.   Why does dis-tance make us   wise?   You were the song

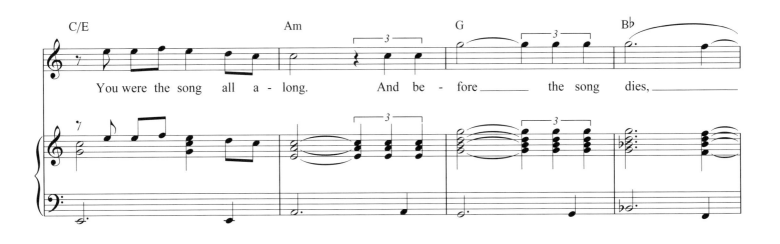

all a - long.   And be - fore _____ the song dies, _____

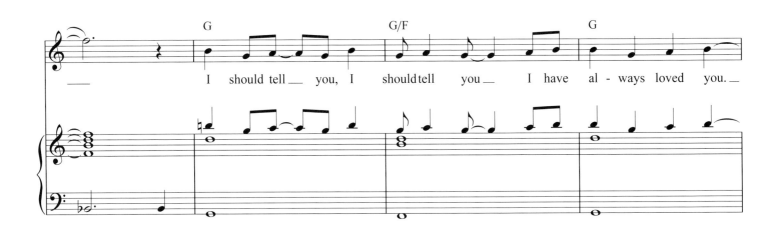

____   I should tell __ you, I should tell you __ I have al - ways loved you. __

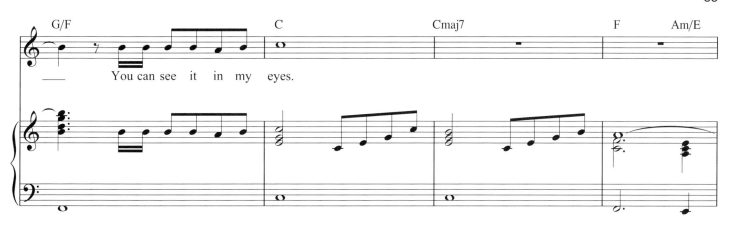

You can see it in my eyes.

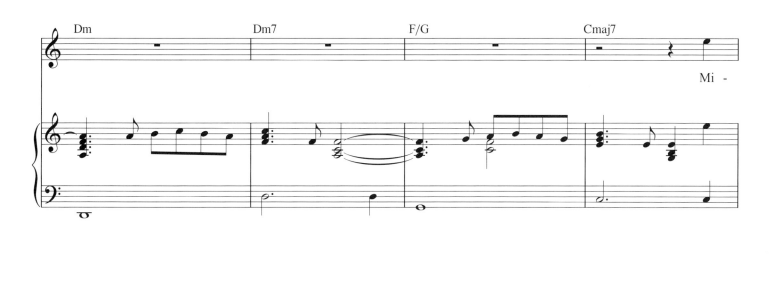

Mi -

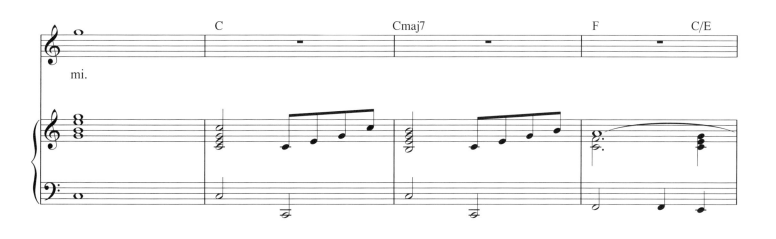

mi.

WHEN WORDS FAIL
from *Shrek the Musical*

Words and Music by Jeanine Tesori
and David Lindsay-Abaire

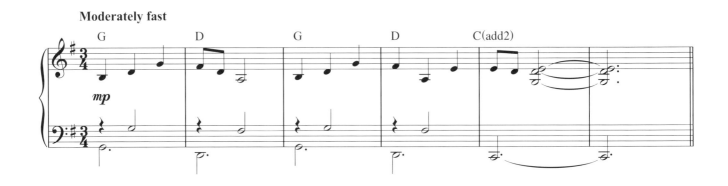

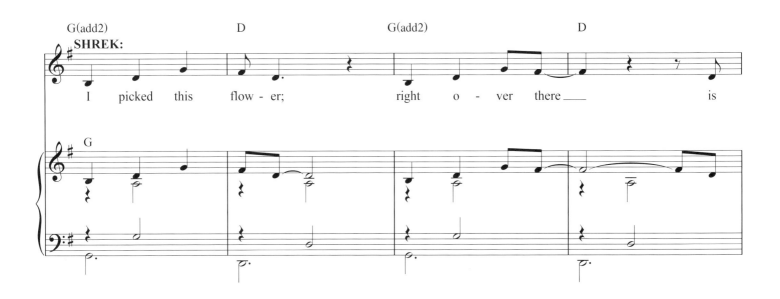

DANCING THROUGH LIFE

from the Broadway Musical *Wicked*

Music and Lyrics by
Stephen Schwartz

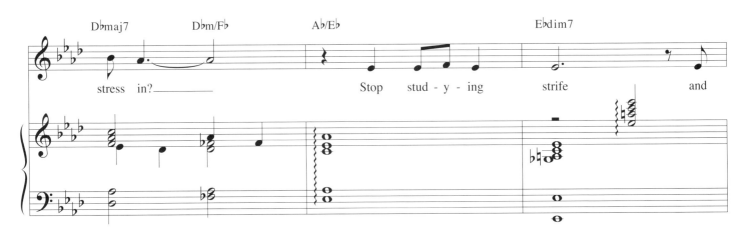

stress in?_____ Stop stud - y - ing strife and

Pop "Dance beat"

learn to live 'the un - ex - am - ined life'"..._____

mp legato

With pedal

Danc - ing through life,___

skim - ming the sur - face, glid - ing where turf__ is smooth._____

BOY FALLS FROM THE SKY

from *Spider-Man: Turn Off the Dark*

Music by U2
Lyrics by Bono and The Edge

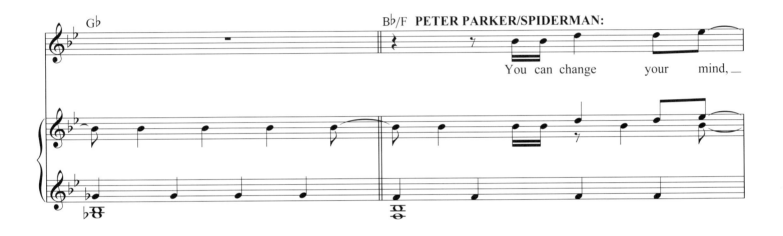

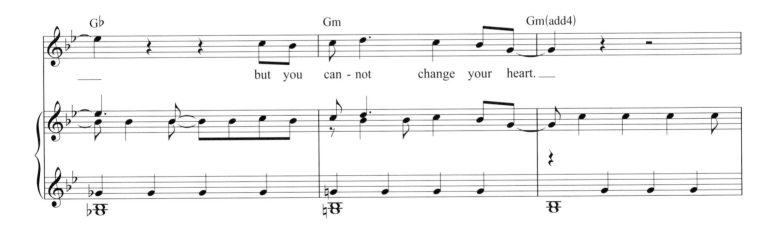

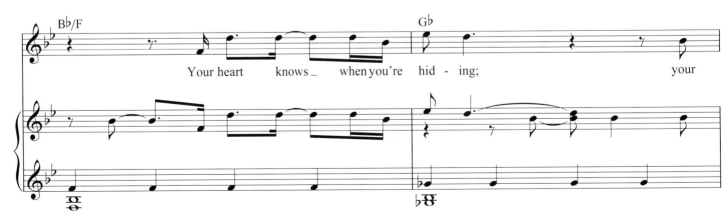

boy fall from the sky. ___

You will al-ways be in front of me, ___ e-ven as I dis-ap-pear from ___ view, ___

___ for I have done ___ not a sin-gle ___ thing ___ with-

be - lieve, _____ be - lieve, _____ be - lieve, _____

_____ be - lieve, _____ be - lieve, _____ ow!

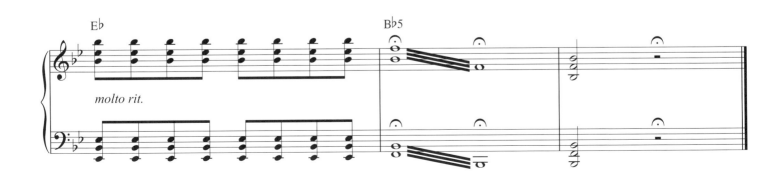

molto rit.

ALL THAT'S KNOWN

from *Spring Awakening*

Music by Duncan Sheik
Lyrics by Steven Sater

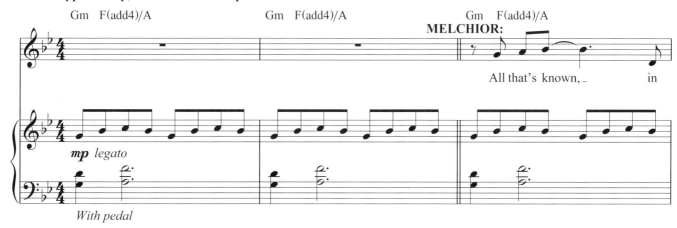

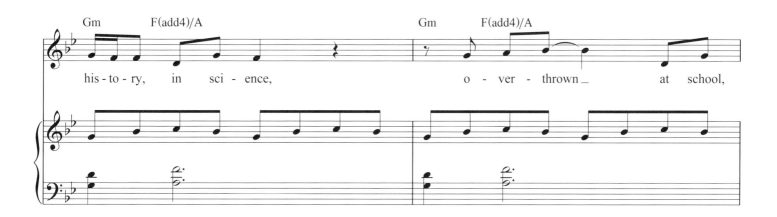

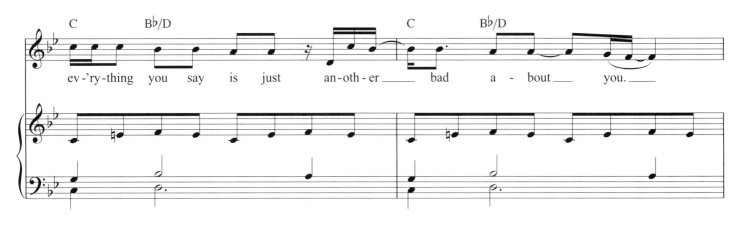

ev-'ry-thing you say is just an-oth-er ___ bad a - bout ___ you. ___

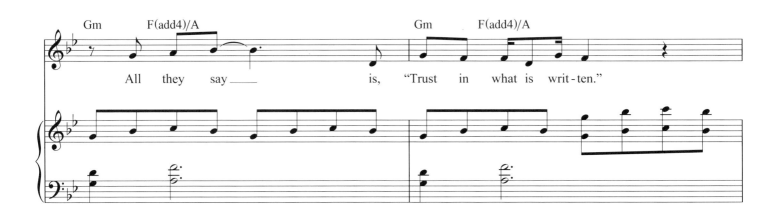

All they say ___ is, "Trust in what is writ-ten."

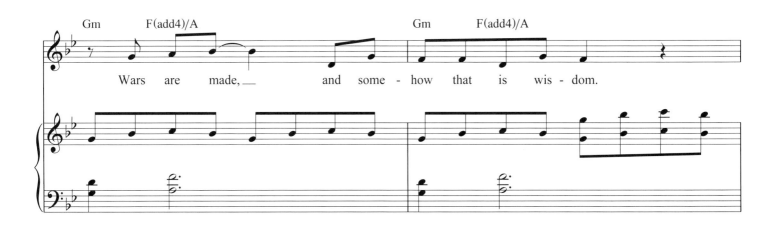

Wars are made, ___ and some - how that is wis - dom.

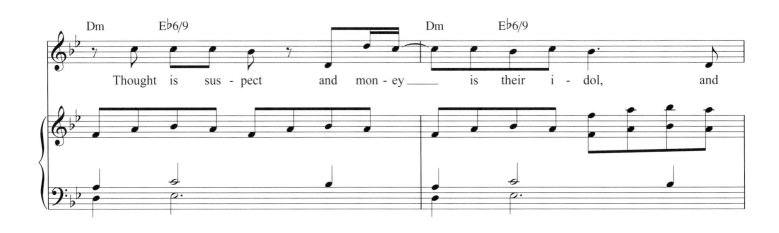

Thought is sus - pect and mon-ey ___ is their i - dol, and

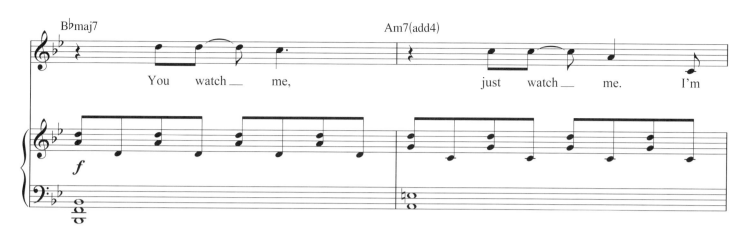

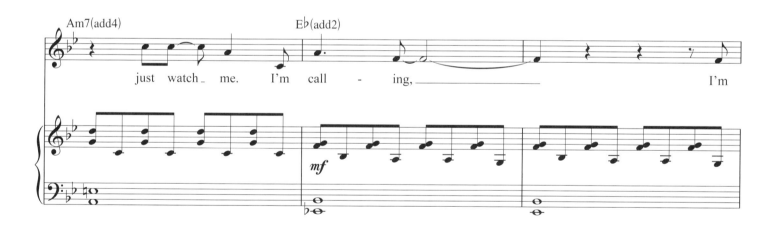

LEFT BEHIND

from *Spring Awakening*

Music by Duncan Sheik
Lyrics by Steven Sater

GET ME WHAT I NEED

from the Broadway Musical *13*

Music and Lyrics by
Jason Robert Brown

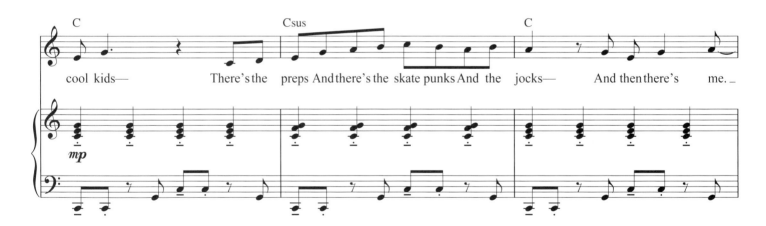

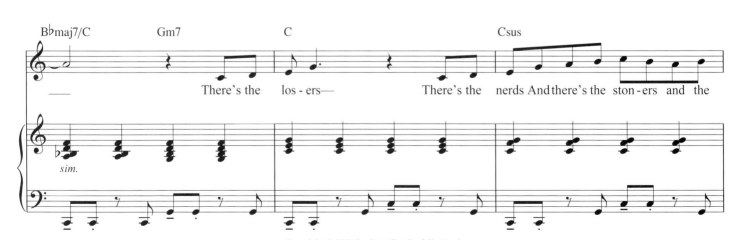

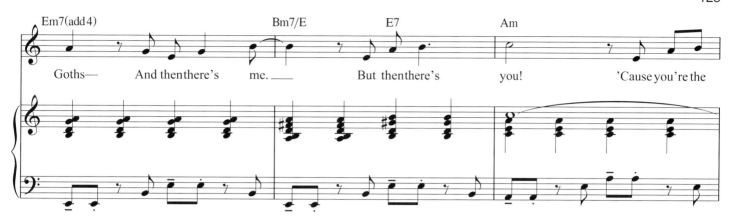

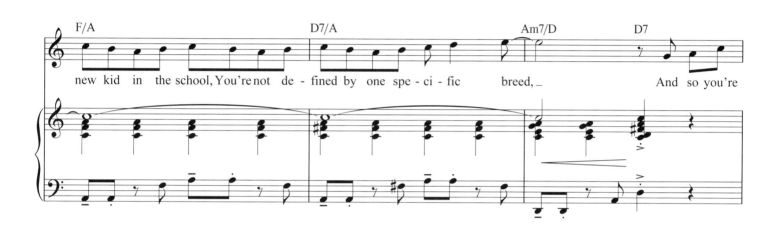

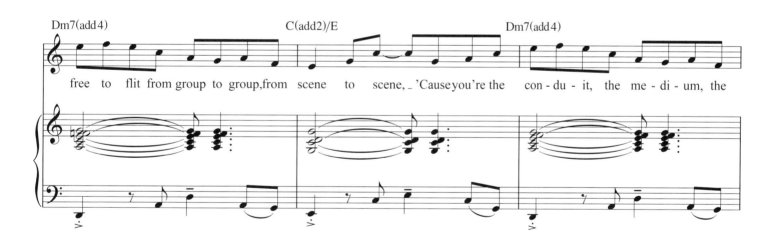

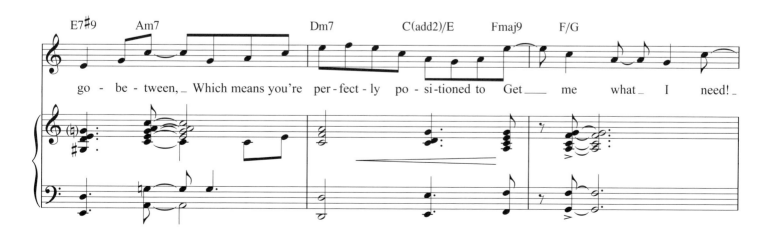

They don't

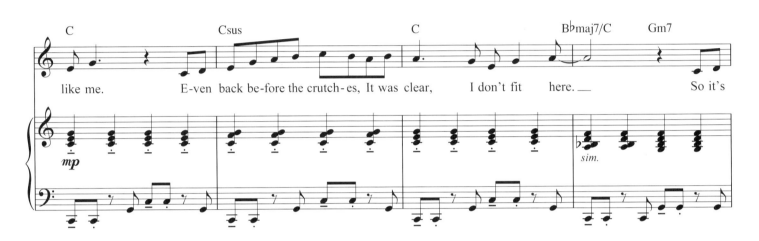

like me. E-ven back be-fore the crutch-es, It was clear, I don't fit here.___ So it's

hope-less, I can't walk right up to Ken-dra and say, "Hey." She'd run a - way.___ But look at

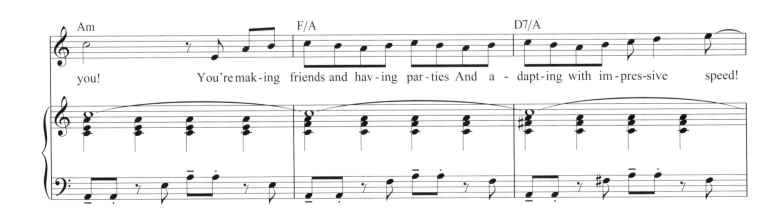

you! You're mak-ing friends and hav-ing par-ties And a - dapt-ing with im-pres-sive speed!

prob- lem: Ev - 'ry min - ute, ev - 'ry sec - ond that I wait Might be too late. __

__ So let's face it: If I ev - er had a chance, the time is

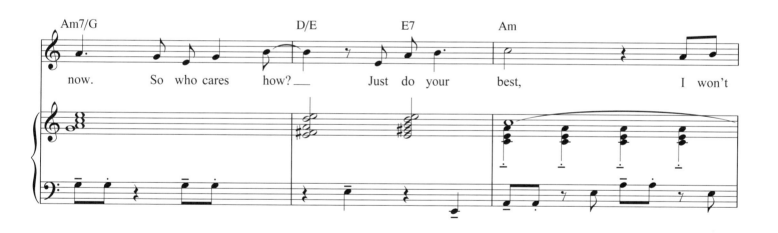

now. So who cares how? __ Just do your best, I won't

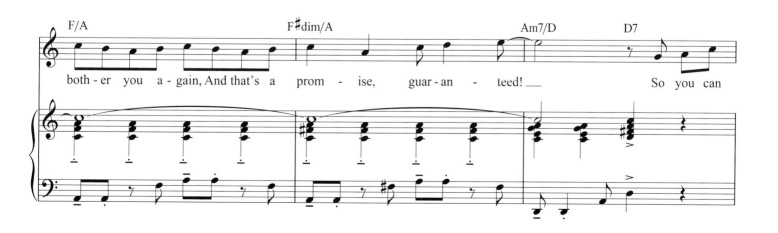

both - er you a - gain, And that's a prom - ise, guar - an - teed! __ So you can

HERE I COME
from the Broadway Musical *13*

Music and Lyrics by
Jason Robert Brown

WHAT DO I NEED WITH LOVE
from *Thoroughly Modern Millie*

Music by Jeanine Tesori
Lyrics by Dick Scanlan

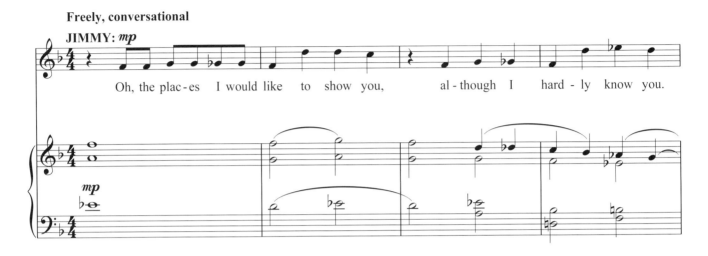

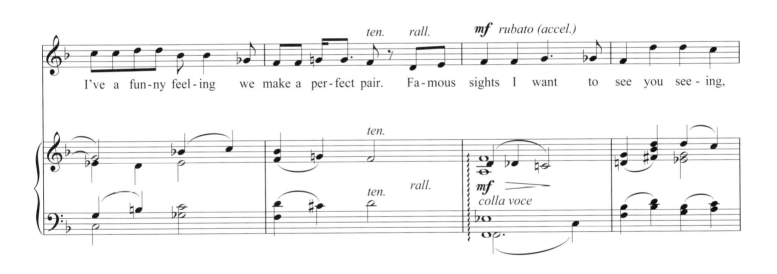

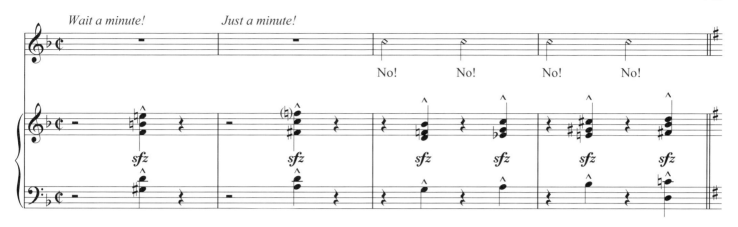

Wait a minute!   *Just a minute!*

No!   No!   No!   No!

A tempo - swingy, in 2

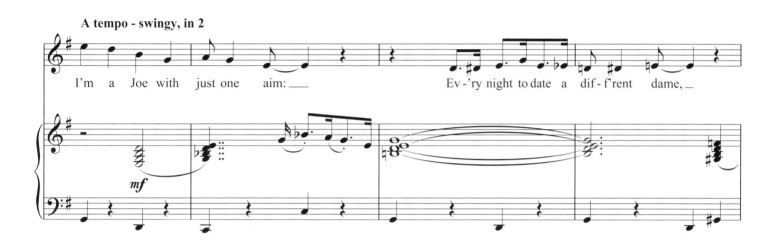

I'm a Joe with just one aim:____ Ev-'ry night to date a dif-f'rent dame,____

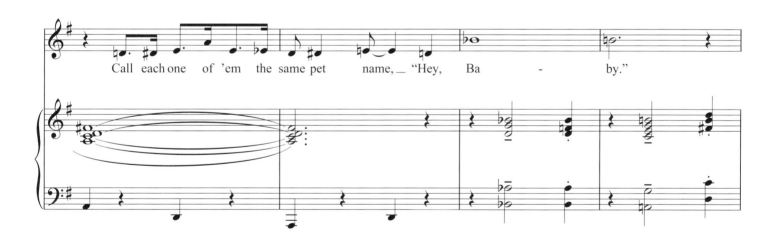

Call each one of 'em the same pet name,__ "Hey, Ba - by."

In a row I have my ducks.____ Loads of gals to give me loads of yucks.__

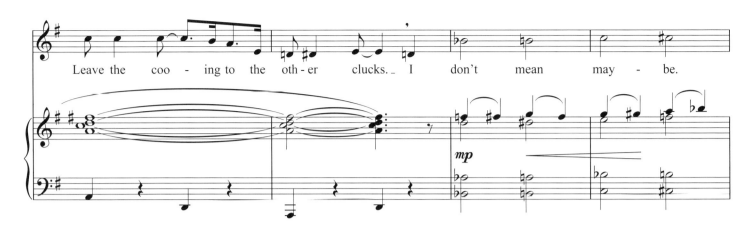

Leave the coo - ing to the oth - er clucks. _ I don't mean may - be.

Got it good. _ What do I need _ with love?

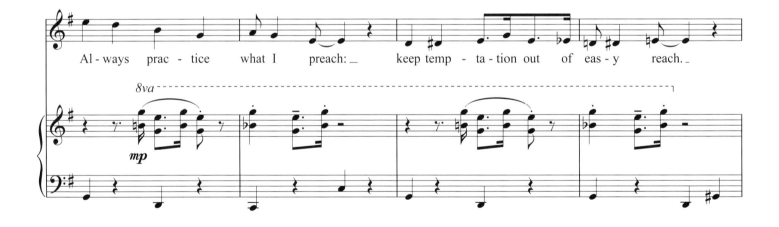

Al - ways prac - tice what I preach: _ keep temp - ta - tion out of eas - y reach. _

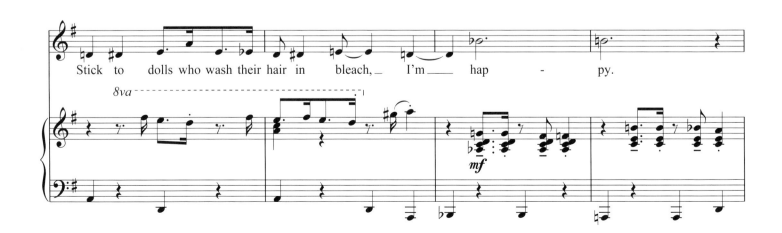

Stick to dolls who wash their hair in bleach, _ I'm ___ hap - py.

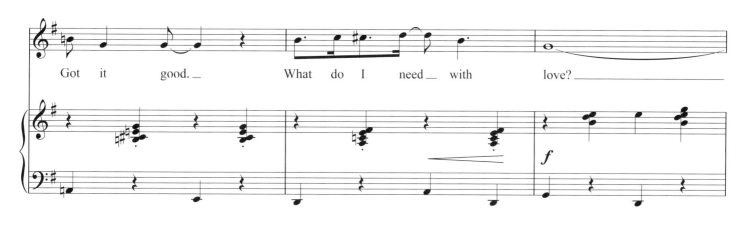

Got it good. ___ What do I need ___ with love? ___

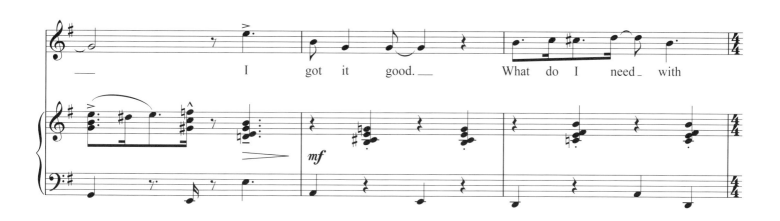

___ I got it good. ___ What do I need ___ with

Double time feel - Straight 8ths

"Jolson"

love? ___ Skip the vows and

all that rot. ___ Tell the min - is - ter that "I ___ do" ___ not.

MY UNFORTUNATE ERECTION

from *The 25th Annual Putnam County Spelling Bee*

Words and Music by
William Finn

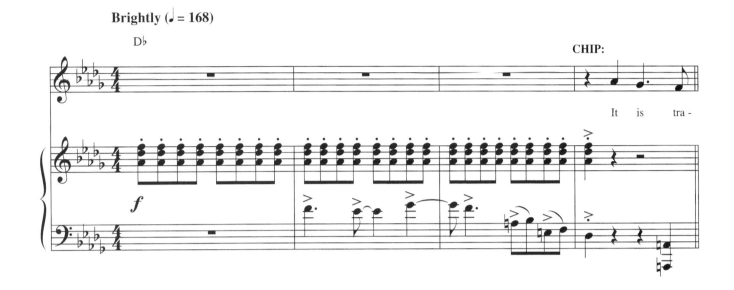

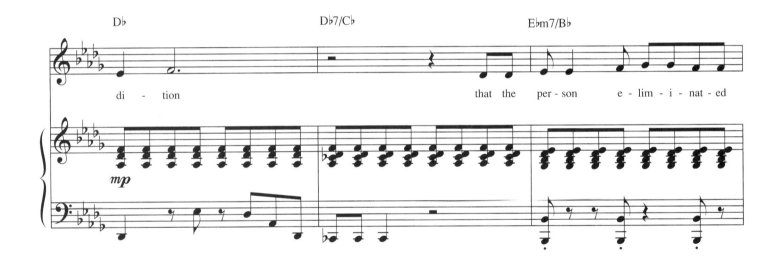

I'LL BE HERE
from *The Wild Party*

Words and Music by
Andrew Lippa

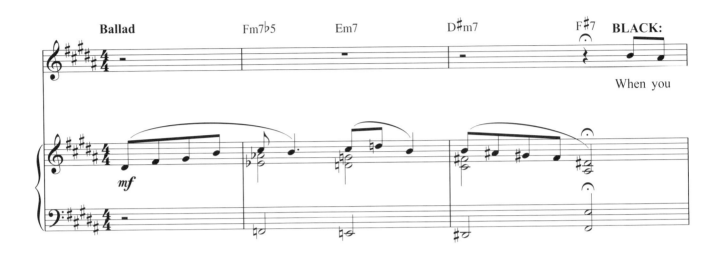

ONE KNIGHT
from the Broadway Musical *Wonderland*

Music by Frank Wildhorn
Lyrics by Jack Murphy

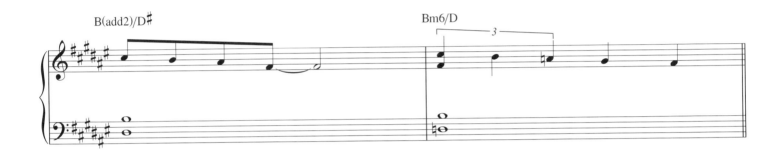

Give me a drag-on I can slay. Just say the word_ and I'll o-bey.

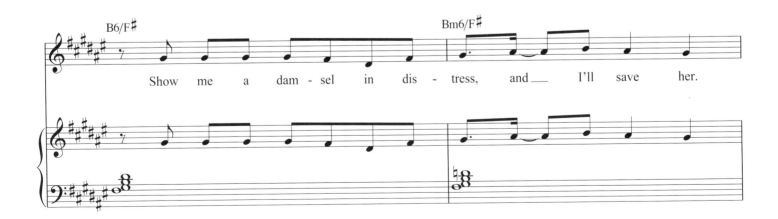

Show me a dam-sel in dis-tress, and _ I'll save her.

If there's a mis-sion, I'm your man; throw in a la-dy if you can.

Though I __ am not Lan - ce - lot, I'll __ be brav - er.

I'll rush in __ to save __ the day. It - 'll look __ good on __ my ré -

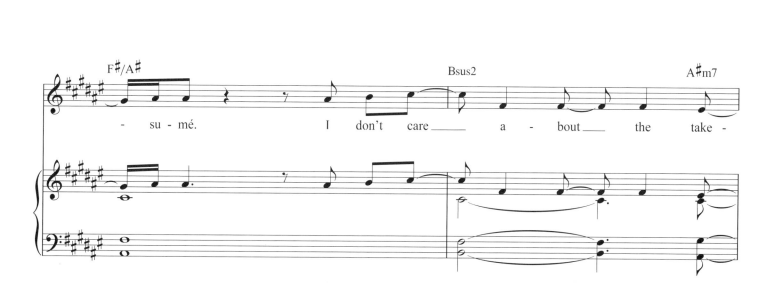

- su - mé. I don't care __ a - bout __ the take -

You'll nev-er find ____ an-oth-er one ____ ____ like me. And e-ven if____ you ev-er do, ____ ____ show _ me one knight _ who will _ be half as true.

Now, listen here... No mat-ter where you wan-na go,

BEETHOVEN DAY

from *You're a Good Man, Charlie Brown*

Words and Music by
Andrew Lippa

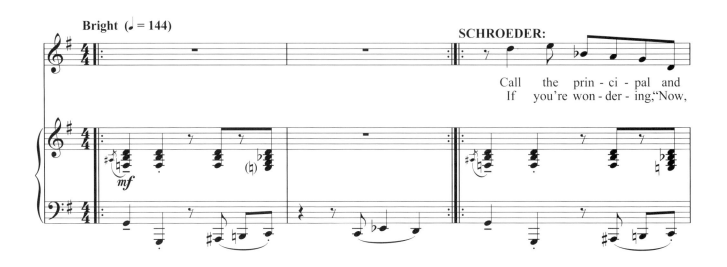

Bee-tho-ven Day! A pol-y-phon-ic jum - ble. A hum-ble ded-i-ca - tion as we

stand up and say:___ Hoo - ray, Bee - tho - ven, Hoo - ray!___

Let's im-a-gine it, that glo-ri-ous hour.___ Filled with e-mo-tion, yet in -